ADVANCED AVIATION MODELLING

Compendium Modelling Manuals
Volume 2

Series Editor: Jerry Scutts

COMPENDIUM

Compendium Modelling Manuals

Advanced Aviation Modelling

This edition published by Compendium Publishing Ltd,
5 Gerrard Street, London,
W1V 7LJ

Printed in the UK
Designed by Compendium Design and Production

A CIP catalogue record for this book is available from the
British Library

ISBN 1 902579 05 4

For further information about any other books in this series
please write to

The Sales Manager

Compendium Publishing, 5 Gerrard Street, London, W1V 7LJ
Tel   0171 287 4570
Fax 0171 494 0583

SUPERDETAILING AEROPLANES

No attempt has been made to specify the brands of paint used throughout this book. The basic mixes are, as indicated, much to the modeller's individual choice based on local availability of paints and inks as well as the reference material used. Ranges of oil-based enamel and water-based acrylic paints and inks suitable for use on polystyrene plastic are available at kit retail outlets in most countries.

A veritable avalanche of literature, from magazines to weighty in-depth books - not to mention videos - confronts the modeller these days and ideally it should be a spur towards achieving a high standard in model construction and finishing. The other side to the coin is the danger of the individual being overwhelmed by the implied need for superdetailing in every phase of model building. While this is not everyone's idea of a recreational hobby, manufacturers are increasingly catering for this end of the market by ever-more sophisticated kits. But assuming that customising kits using some basic materials is still valid both approaches can be blended, as we show in the following pages.

SUPERDETAILING USING PHOTO-ENGRAVING

The A-10 'Warthog' is well known for its combat role in the Gulf War; camouflaged in the greens and greys intended for operations in Europe, the machine stood out against the sands of the desert. Numerous Iraqi tanks and soft-skinned vehicles were destroyed by A-10s, which were also involved in a notorious 'friendly fire' incident against British forces.

Our A-10 is to 1/48 scale by Tamiya with superdetailing added by using the Verlinden kit. This latter consists of resin and brass-etched items for improving the cockpit, control panels and underwing hard-points. As a basic reference we used the Verlinden A-10 monograph.

To complete the detailing, some custom-made pieces are required; in order to fit the side consoles the corresponding panels have to be cut out. The best way to do this is by drilling a series of holes from the inside, following the kit panel lines.

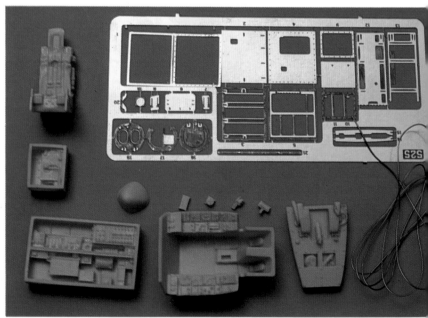

The Verlinden A-10 conversion kit offers useful cockpit additions to use in conjunctie with kit parts.

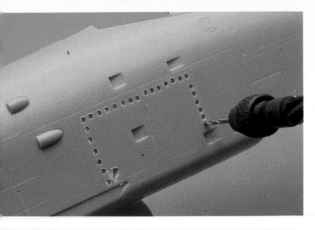

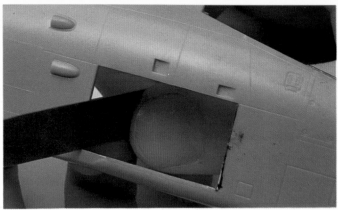

ut out a panel, first weaken it by drilling a series of holes.

The edges are cleaned up with a scalpel, file and sandpaper ensuring that the correct shape is retained.

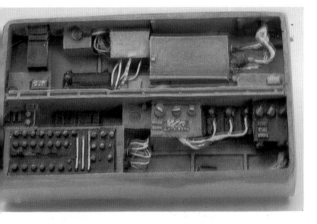

...per wire is used to detail the control panels, which are ...ted before assembly.

It is useful to add an internal framework support for customised parts.

...e the unwanted sections have ...n removed, trim with a knife and ...sh off with a flat file. Some small ...es of plastic can now be fitted as ...ame to support the resin parts. ...per wire to simulate the wiring ...ble on the full-size aircraft can ... be added at this stage. Cockpit ...rior painting can now be ...pleted along with the insides of ... engine nacelles.

...our colours, brown, black, ochre ... grey, are applied to the airframe ...g an airbrush in steady longitu-...al sweeps to create a feathered ...e.

...he engines and exhausts are ...n a base coat of metallic grey ...r which is applied two layers of ...k. Unpainted areas shown will ... be painted dark brown with ...ers left in the metallic grey plastic ...d to mould the kit.

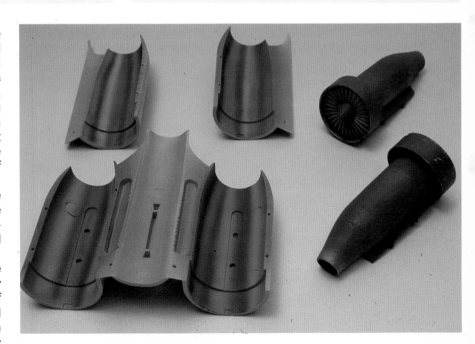

The engine bay interiors are painted before assembly. A mix of black, brown and silver is used to highlight engine detail.

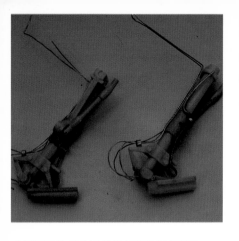

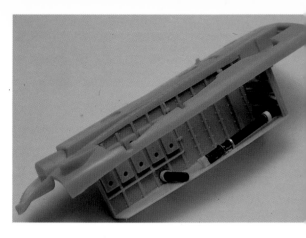

Copper wire in different thicknesses complements the authentic look of the landing gear and wheel wells.

Plastic rod detail added to the cannon bay.

ADDING DETAILS WITH WIRE

Compared to the landing gear fitted to most Second World War aircraft, modern warplanes such as the A-10 seem to have gained considerably in complexity. Oleo legs and wheel bays are full of pipes, tubes, cables and rods, some of which can be duplicated on the Tamiya model. Plastic card and rod can be well utilised to fill out the rather bare wheel wells, giving a more three-dimensional effect.

The multi-barrel M61 cannon can also be improved by drilling out and leaving the inside hollow to take a plastic barrel. Air cooling holes also be opened up and the tip each of the seven revolving bar can be made up to show these protruding from the cann mounting.

The A-10's ejector seat con pretty well finished although so

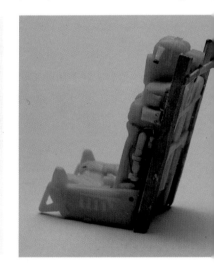

Holes are drilled in the gun muzzle and the bay is detailed with wire and plastic tubing.

The ejection seat complete with guide rails and other cockpit detail items.

The new instrument panels are positioned and painted.

detail can still be added. We deci to add the rails upon which the s would slide during an ejection cable for the compressed air bo and some headrest 'extras'. In ad tion, the hydraulic power unit beh the seat was built up as a th dimensional item, this area be moulded merely as a flat tray i gral with the seat back.

The new cockpit instrument pa also comes as a single 'flat' item needs building out in appropr places with 0.3 and 0.5-mm pla card shaped and cut to size. Grou together below the main pa these additional panels look q realistic even though the instrum dials are quite small.

The cockpit has been painted shades of grey, green and bro mixed with white in areas such the seat upholstery and belts wh

...h the cockpit interior complete and painted, the fuselage
...ves can be joined.

*View of the completed cockpit showing the revised instrument
panel, consoles and additions to the ejector seat.*

...h new resin parts added, the A-10 cockpit looks more
...vincing compared to merely assembling the basic kit parts
...ich lack depth.

*View of the left side of the model showing shades of red-
yellow and bright green on the compressed air bottle.*

a light beige in colour. On the
side of the fuselage below the
...kpit the crew entry ladder door
...given more detail than supplied
...the kit. Once the cockpit inte-
..., nosewheel well and doors have
...n painted and the nosewheel leg
...ched, both halves of the fuse-
...e are glued together.

MAKING THE PANELS STAND OUT

One of the most common problems
when filling seam lines, gaps and
sink marks with body putty is that
scribed or raised detail on the
surface of the model will be covered
or sanded away during the

smoothing-down process. Lines that
start but appear not to end
anywhere can spoil the overall effect
of an otherwise well-finished model.
Restoring embossed surface detail is
difficult, the only real option being
to stick minute strips of plastic to the
surface to maintain raised lines.
With engraved surface detail the

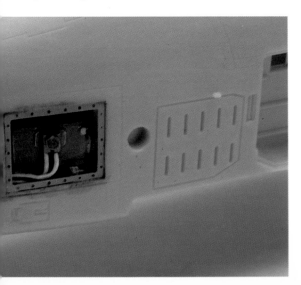

*Don't overlook
other small panels
with which the
fuselage of this
aircraft is covered.*

*Areas such as the
fuel filling points
are nicely detailed
on the resin and
brass accessory
parts.*

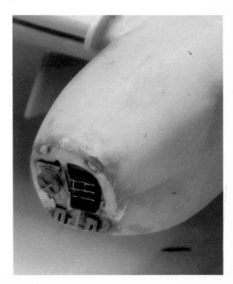

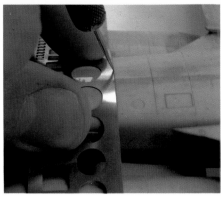

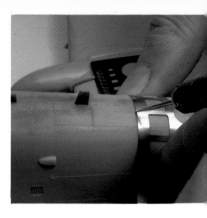

The jet exhausts are painted in a mix of metallic grey and brown.

Filler inevitably gets into panel lines and other small surface detail.

Make good any panel lines which hav[e] been covered with filler with a rule an[d] punch. Verlinden supply useful flexibl[e] metal templates for this purpose.

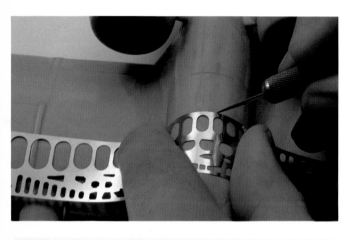

The templates conform to the most challenging curves on the model and others are available, if required.

Exceptionally good restoration of lost panel lines is possible with the templates, with no unsightly half-erased detail that often marred models in the past.

Prior to painting[,] cockpit, wells and all o[ther] panels are secu[rely] masked[.]

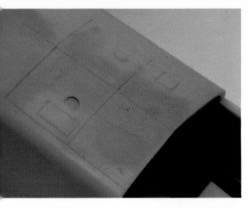

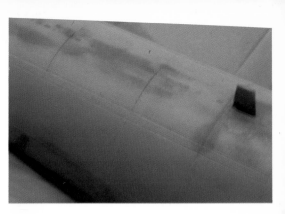

Putty covers all the joints, resulting in a continuous surface.

The filler is smoothed off with No 600 grade wet and dry sandpaper.

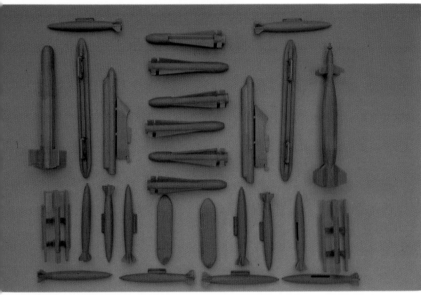

...erous weapons options are possible with the A-10 and a comprehensive range of ...siles and bombs is supplied in the kit.

greens and greys, was chosen for aircraft operating with Nato forces and used in combat during the Gulf War. Using acrylics and inks we followed the painting process explained previously, having masked wells and open hatches with paper and adhesive tape, the cockpit area with Maskol and the engine exhaust with tissue.

As this A-10 scheme 'wraps around' the entire airframe, a base colour of matt light olive green is applied first. Camouflage can be applied at this stage if the airbrush is loaded and ready to use, the advantage being that the feathered edges to the different shades can be reproduced before each is fully dry. Spray from close in with low air flow. If hand painting is to be employed masks will be required with the camouflage edges painted first and then filled in.

...ion is far easier in that a punch ...rule can be used to continue ...and panel lines over areas of ... Where a surface is curved ...Verlinden photo-engraved ...lates are invaluable, as they are ...flexible yet rigid enough to hold ...ace. They are taped firmly to the ...ace to be scribed by adhesive ...or held in place for new grooves ...e made with a punch or sharp ...t. Usefully, the Verlinden kit ...ides a single template for 1/72 ...work and one for 1/48 scale, ...with different shapes and of ...se, sizes.

...TING AND DECORATION

...aircraft subject to numerous ...rimental camouflage patterns, ...A-10 has had schemes based on ...es, creams, light greys, earth ...ns and spots of green and ...n. A more traditional pattern ...isting of large areas of dark

Although applying putty might seem tedious, the finished results are well worth the effort.

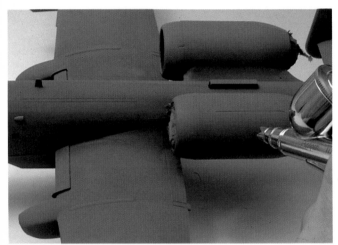

Paints used to finish the model are acrylic, matt green being our first coat.

A second green with a bluish tinge is created by mixing sea blue and matt green to build up the camouflage pattern.

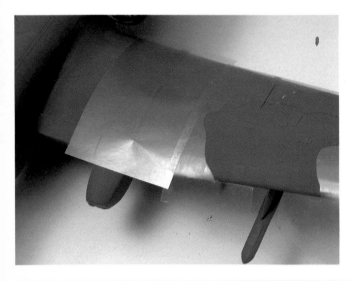

Both airbrush and hand painting require that the different camouflage areas be masked off.

Draw the outline of the colour segments before filling them with paint.

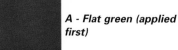

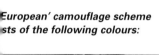

A - Flat green (applied first)

B - Sea blue (40%) and flat green (60%) mixed

C - Medium grey

D - Sepia.

European' camouflage scheme
sts of the following colours:

The sea blue, a 40-60% ratio of sea blue and matt green respectively, is applied next, with the Neutral Grey going on last. Method is as before with adhesive templates being used where two colours meet. With overall camouflaging complete, weathering effects are tackled using in this case the Verlinden 'Lock-On' No 7 on the A-10. This publication clearly illustrates the 'used' look of removable panels, control surfaces, the area around fuel fillers and so on. Sepia and grey inks were used on our model to simulate the wear and tear of operational service. Practice with airbrush and masks will indicate the degree of dirt and grime to apply to various areas of the airframe.

For the grey shade USAAF World War II Neutral Grey is a close match.

To feather the edges of each camouflage shade, masks need not be used if a very fine spray is maintained.

eroplane is
oletely painted
 for the final
es with inks.

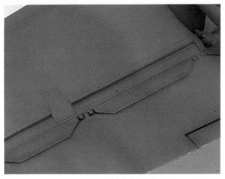

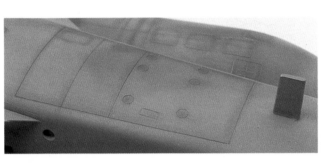

Weathering a model convincingly can be a challenge. A light touch is needed when spraying to ensure that the effect is not overdone.

Ailerons and flaps are treated to give an authentic 'well used' look.

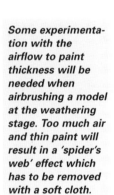

When lightening or darkening paint to simulate fading around panels that are often removed, the weathered areas should be well blended into the surrounding shade and not be too obvious.

Some experimentation with the airflow to paint thickness will be needed when airbrushing a model at the weathering stage. Too much air and thin paint will result in a 'spider's web' effect which has to be removed with a soft cloth.

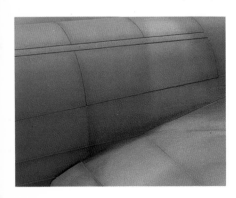

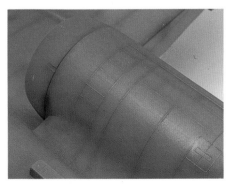

Some angles and contours can be difficult to cover well if the airbrush is not completely clean or the paint is not well mixed.

Airbrushing will generally cope with most weathering although rubbing on graphite or pastel dust can be effective in some areas.

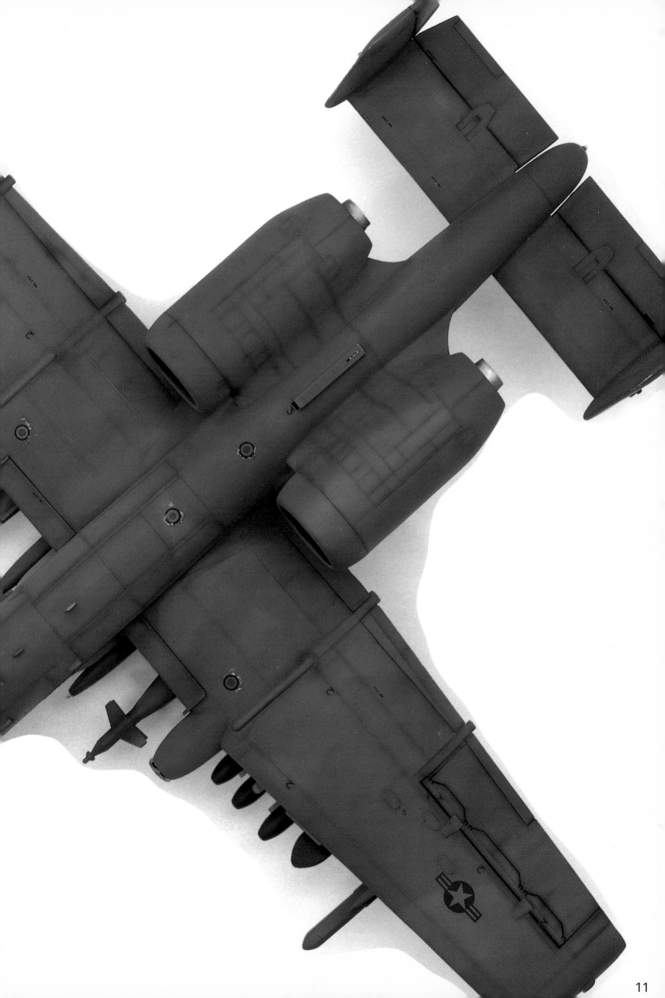

SUPERDETAILING AT YOUR FINGERTIPS

MiG-29 FULCRUM IN 1/32 SCALE

Having previously described (in volume one) the ease with which a 1/72 scale MiG-29 can be assembled and airbrushed, we progress to a much larger kit of the same aircraft in 1/32 scale. Made by Revell, this kit is large enough to enable superdetailing to be carried out that much easier. Some experience with a range of tools useful in modelling is naturally an advantage, as are good references to the full-size aircraft. We consulted the Aerofax Extra No 2: MiG-29 by Jay Miller and Japanese publications that include photos of the aircraft taken at the 1989 Paris Air Show.

Both publications include n 'round the clock' and close-up photos of the MiG-29 and MiG-2

Given that most modellers unable to spend more than a hours at a time on a project, it been estimated that to complete of this size to the desired standa finish will take about two mont phased work. Planning each sta

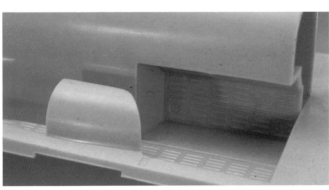

The kit wheel wells are rather bare of essential 'plumbing' and in fact are too shallow to enclose the wheels and oleo legs.

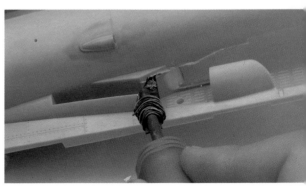

As the wells have to be enlarged, a soldering iron can be us to quickly melt away the plastic.

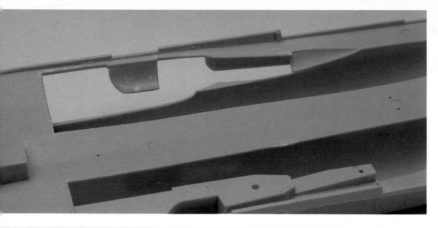

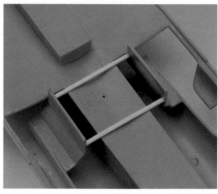

Once the rough edges of the widened wheel wells have been smoothed down, new plasticard walls are glued inside the fuselage.

Spacer strips are located to hold the new plasticard sections.

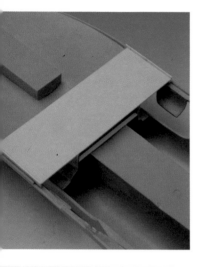

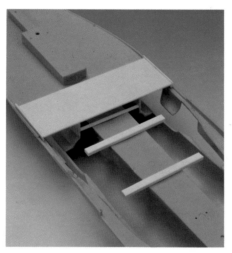

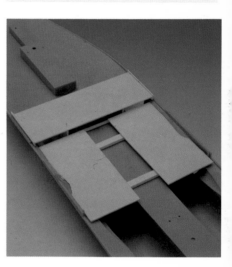

plasticard sections are needed, cut to width of the fuselage.

Plastic strips are required to support the base of the wells.

Strengthening new parts as much as possible is very important.

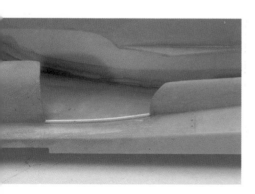

Strips are also positioned to follow the curvature of the fuselage.

A view of the new sections in situ.

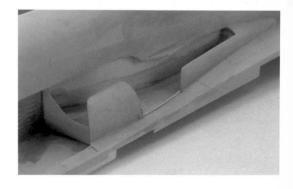

before recommended.

The main phases of work on this particular kit are to detail the wheel wells and landing gear, the cockpit and the fuselage and wings in general, which includes adding small aerials, intakes and other tiny items.

Among the materials needed are: plasticard sheets in sizes 0.3, 0.5 and 0.7mm; copper wire; tubing in various thicknesses; plastic rod; brass sheeting and epoxy putty.

WORKING PROCEDURE

Before any detail work can begin the mainwheel wells have to be enlarged. Each kit wall is removed and built up with new plasticard sections with suitable strengthening and additional bracing. The nose-wheel well needs to be totally reconstructed.

Comparison photographs of the real MiG-29 will determine the extent of rebuilding necessary using the kit

Small plastic strip is remarkably effective even if only partially visible when the model is completed.

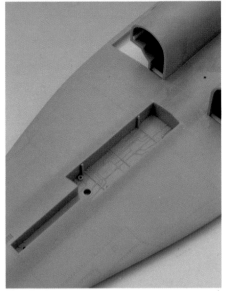

As moulded, the nosewheel well has insufficient depth

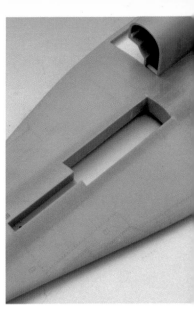

New plasticard walls are added, using the kit sections as supports.

parts, and the degree of extra detail to incorporate.

WIRING

A mass of wiring covers the inside of each wheel well and to reproduce enough of this to make the end result convincing, tubing and wire is needed. The insulation material which binds the wiring together is glued in place with cyanoacrylate, preferably before each well section is located on the model. Small clamps, location points and so forth are reproduced with plasticard, rod and, where appropriate, small pieces of polystrene plastic from the kit sprues.

The work done on the wheel wells results in a convincing impression of depth and complexity. Close scrutiny of photographs will be invaluable in making the customised parts to the correct shape and size.

Profile of a MiG-29 of the Czechoslovak Air Force.

With our modifications, the walls are extended by about one centimeter.

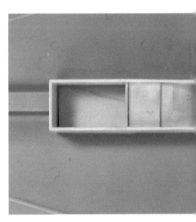

The well is detailed by incorporating additions that are clearly visible in the reference material.

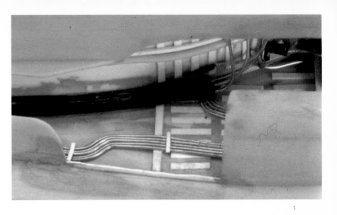

Riveted plates are simulated by plasti-card and cable retainers are reproduced with small plastic strips bent to shape.

Plastic and metal tubing reproduces piping and ducting very convincingly

Cable looms need to be glued prior to locating them on the model.

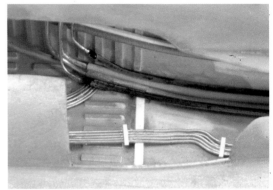

...erences will show that the MiG's ...eel wells have different patterns of ...les and wiring.

The walls of the adjacent inboard wells contain a mass of wiring looms and cables.

The sheer complexity of modern fighter wheel wells is soon appreciated - at least four thicknesses of material will be needed for 're-wiring' the model.

5918

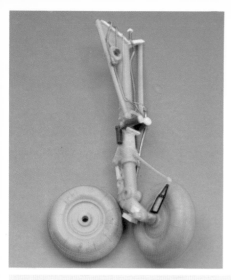

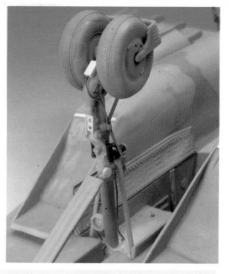

The kit nosewheel with hydraulic lines, links and other small details added.

Absence of detail in the original kit mouldings facilitates detailing.

Diagram of the MiG-29 instrument panel, left and right consoles and the control column.

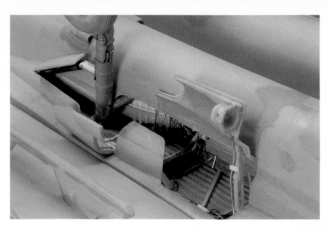

Copper wire glued with cyanoacrylate, thin metal sheet and short lengths of plastic tubing all go to make up the auxiliary items attached to the oleo legs.

LANDING GEAR

Small additional pieces are added to each of the main oleo legs, a process actually helped by the manufacturer leaving most of these parts 'clean'. Had detail been moulded in, some of it would have to be removed before additions can be made. Cables, lines, brackets, clamps and small cylinders can thus be fashioned and positioned without difficulty.

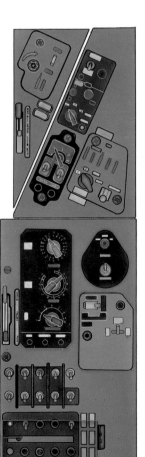

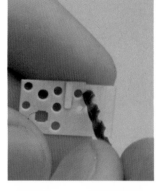

The kit instrument panel is covered by thin plasticard. The shape of each instrument is drawn on the card after marking the centres and individually cutting out with a drill or file, the square faces being created with an appropriately-shaped file. Strips are added to build out the panel where appropriate.

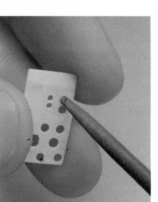

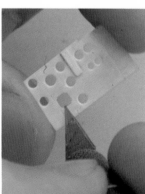

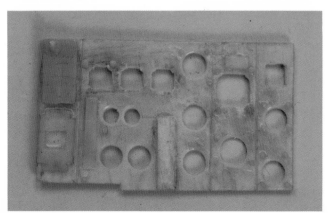

The finished instrument panel shown at three times actual size. Any surface irregularities are filled with putty and smoothed off later.

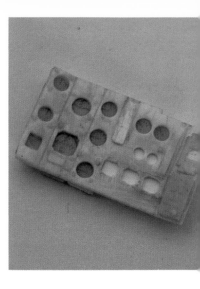

The kit instrument panels are used to provide firm anchors for the new instrument display.

The right side console has to be almost entirely custom-made using suitably thick plasti-card.

It is advisable to use files, wet & dry sandpaper and a punch to accurately reproduce the necessary additional parts for the oleo legs, bearing in mind the limitations of scale. While adding detail, the beacon and its wiring located in each well should not be overlooked.

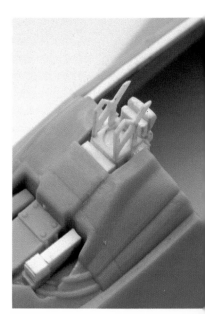

The right hand instrument panel section is quite complex and requires the addition of several new sections fashioned from thin plasticard and strips.

Viewed from either side the new gun-sight support bracket looks quite authentic.

...ew of the model's upper ...aces showing the ...erous tiny sensors, ...es and antenna.

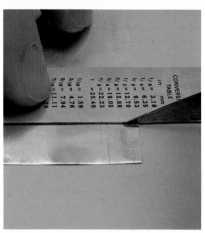

Behind the seat the electrical junction box should be detailed and given a raised support. A second smaller box is made to go into the resulting cavity.

Brass sheet is used for the support, cut with the aid of a previously prepared template.

A metal rule and flat-headed pliers are used to bend the brass component int position.

The box made from brass sheet - which has the same look and thickness as photo-etched parts - and plasticard is positioned behind the seat, set low enough to ensure that the canopy will slide over it.

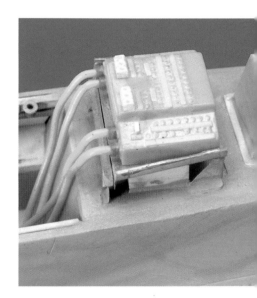

COCKPIT INTERIOR

Because of the complexity of the cockpit area, it is convenient to divide the remedial work into two parts. A start is made at the front where the gunsight and instrument panel are the main items. Although the kit provides all the essential instrument dials arranged on the panel in approximately the right places, reference photos will show that rather than being 'flat',as in the kit, the panel has raised areas and the glass faces of some analogue instruments are recessed. The kit parts can be used as a guide for a new plasticard panel, suitably adapted to reflect more closely the fittings of the full size aircraft. It is important to measure the area each instrument grouping occupies as the holes drilled in the new panel need to match those in the kit as closely as possible.

A general view of the rear cockpit with added detail including the cables running fro the junction box.

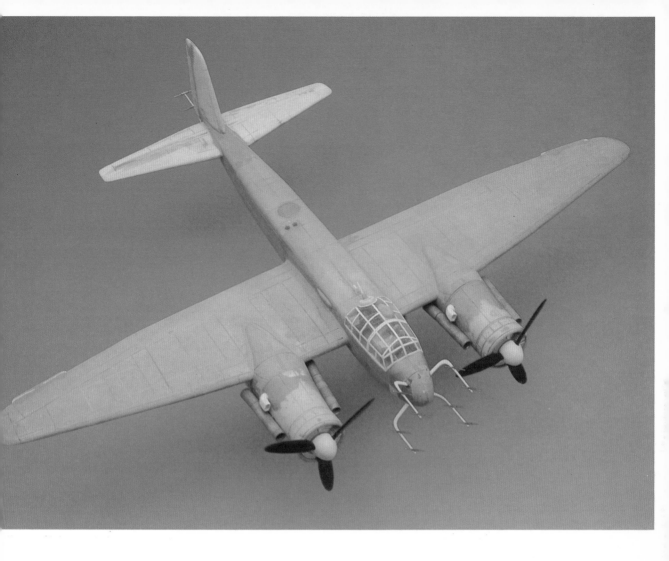

ADVANCED TECHNIQUES

eaders should note that the onversion of the Hobby Craft Inkers Ju 88A-4 (Kit No C1601) included in this olume was carried out before e release of a Ju 88G-6 night ghter (Kit No HC1606) from e same company. The night ghter version essentially corporates all the modified irts covered in this section of e book. It goes without saying at the methods described n generally be applied to umerous other conversions of rcraft kits.

Superdetailing of model kits can encompass numerous advanced techniques, more perhaps than most modellers will need to use. It is however useful to have practical knowledge of such methods as vaccum-forming and adapting plastic parts on a lathe in the event that these skills will come into play at some future date. Most advanced techniques have a practical application and are designed to improve on kit components. They also give the modeller an insight into how plastic kits are made.

SUPERDETAILING A MiG-29 IN 1/32 SCALE

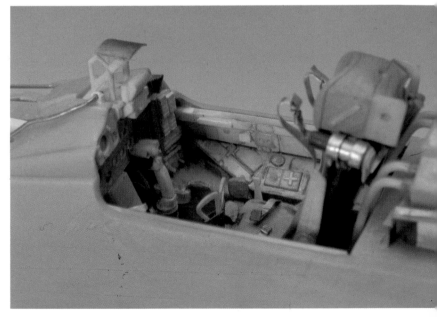

The complexity of the MiG-29's cockpit requires substantial rebuilding using plasticard brass and wire.

Work on this model includes the contruction of a series of instrument consoles built up from small squares of plastic slotted with a triangular needle file to give a three-dimensional effect.

The reflector gunsight on the MiG-29 is a substantial instrument, and to improve the look of it, new component parts are drawn onto 5/10th-in plasticard and cut out with a knife, pre-scribing where appropriate.

The electrical circuit box situated behind the seat is structured on two levels separated by a rack that should be made from 3/10th-in brass sheet, bent and cut with pliers and glued in position with cyanoacrylate. A generous number of control knobs are added to the ones supplied in the kit, the main console also having a bunch of cables added from copper wire.

The control column incorporates several cylinders and a bunch of

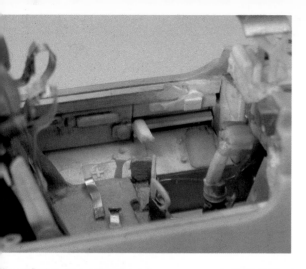

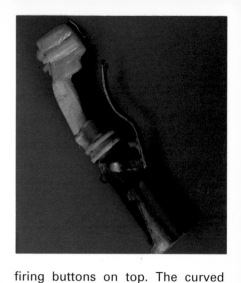

Cockpit side consoles are made entirely from plasti-card using a file and sandpaper.

A new control column was scratch-built using plastic tubing and brass.

...ery basic ejector seat is provided in ...kit and much more detail can be to ...dded.

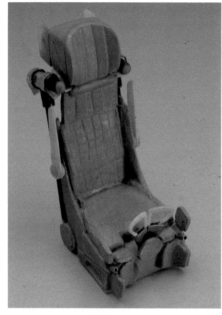

firing buttons on top. The curved shape of the column should be reproduced adding the cylinders supplied in the kit. The lower end of the column was made from plastic tubing with an anchorage point made from brass. The ejector seat is also a very complex structure, that included in the kit being good only as a basis upon which to build detail. Much can be added by the skilled modeller, from the seat upholstery fashioned from body putty to a more accurate ejection handle cut from thin plastic.

Seat belts and buckles are fash-

New parts are carefully measured and made from plastic, brass, tin and epoxy putty.

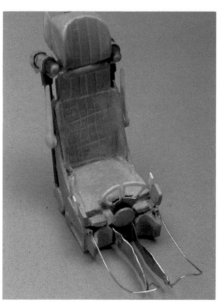

...all discs made with a hollow punch ...re to reproduce appropriately-shaped ...ns on the ejector seat.

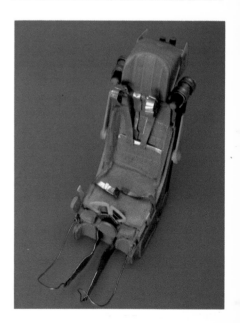

Leg restraints were fashioned from copper wire and tinplate.

Tinplate makes convincing looking-seat belts with buckles in copper wire.

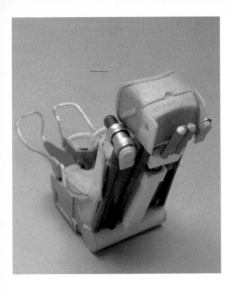

Even with all the new components added, at least twenty per cent of the detail visibl on the real aircraft has not been incorporated.

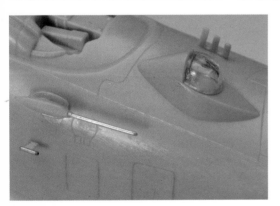

Small intakes on the exterior of the fuselage are made from hypodermic needles, plastic strip and sheet.

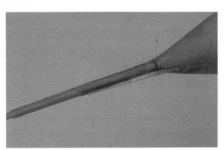

The nose probe has tiny lateral strakes which are made from brass plate.

breaker switches and so on, are situated on the cockpit sidewalls. To reproduce these levers and knobs a substantial number of dowel

Overall view of the superde-tailing carried out on the model.

ioned from tinplate and copper wire to add realism - but modern fighters are like a bottomless well in that no matter how much additional work the modeller does, there is always something more to add. In the case of the MiG-29 the space behind the seat is crammed with cylinders and wiring.

The controls to operate the various weapons carried by the MiG-29, plus the radio knobs, circuit

extra thin aerial mast made from
s plate.

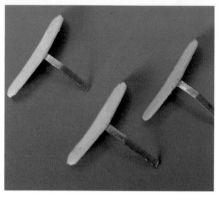

*Cockpit canopy rear-view mirrors made
from plastic and brass plate.*

*Plastic sheet is used to reinforce the
canopy runners.*

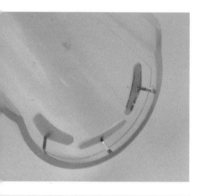

*tion of the rear-view mirrors around
front of the main canopy frame.*

will be required. The controls
made by melting plastic sprue
enough to create a tiny blob to
esent a knob surmounting a
r. Photo-etched brass can be
 for these components which
ave to be very carefully made
 yet strong enough not to break
 as they are positioned.

*The height of the ejector seat will increase slightly when the headrest is detailed so it
is important to ensure that the canopy closes securely and that it is set at the correct
angle when in the open position.*

The external skin of the aircraft, from the nose probe to the rear cockpit area, is covered with sensors and various antennae. These are fashioned from sections of hypodermic needle, small plastic pieces or brass cut to size. The nose probe incorporates small strakes which are also made from brass or plastic.

The radio mast is made from brass, as are the rear-view mirror supports. The mirrors themselves are made from plas-

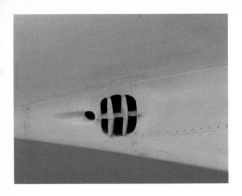

The gun cooling system has thin shields which are made from brass.

The aileron control linkages are moulded solid in the kit and new ones should be made from tubing.

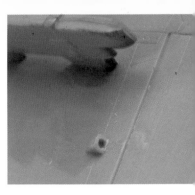

The original linkage is cut away, leav[ing] the locating point clear.

Scratch-built from rod and sheet, new linkages are shaped from a plastic disc.

Holes are drilled in the wing trailing edge to take the static electricity dischargers.

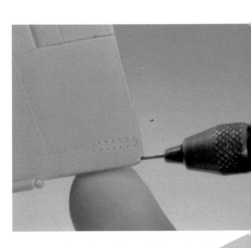

ticard and positioned at the front of the canopy frame, this being reinforced with 5/10th-in plasticard strip.

Creating the additional, invariably small component parts described here does not require sophisticated tools, practically every-

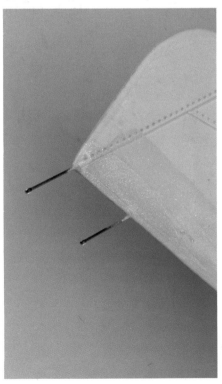

Sections of hypodermic needle are inserted and located with epoxy glue.

Metal needle sections, which have the advantage of bending without breaking, are positioned on the wings and rudders.

General view of the finished MiG-29 showing most of the improvements made to the Revell kit.

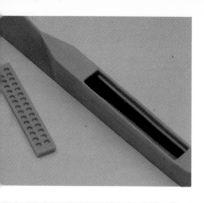

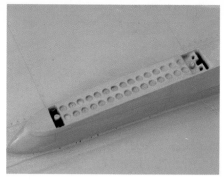

flare launcher fairings are incorrect h in proportions and outline shape.

Plastic sheet is used to contruct new flare launchers which are matched up with the location holes in the kit.

g being possible with a scalpel a needle file. The secret of ccess lies in closely studying the ensions of the part to be made interpreting how best to build it ccurately as possible within the tations of scale. Choosing the t material is important as, even /32 scale, many items are very ll indeed.

or example, the gun gas ersers located around the on muzzle on the MiG-29 were detailed from brass plate; while at first glance this may seem unnecessary as the degree of work done is not easy to see, the detail revealed when the area is closely examined shows admirable attention to detail and the high level of realism the modeller has aimed for. Tackling jobs such as rebuilding the aileron linkages, which is a simple task, results in a model which undoubtedly has

a more authentic look - which goes for all the work described and shown here.

Most aircraft have static dischargers on wing and rudder trailing edges and adding these is again a simple job. Metal needles were used, as plastic will break easily and brass is too soft. Needles cut to length are positioned firmly with epoxy adhesive.

Among the improvements to the MiG-29 kit are the chutes forward of each dorsal fin from which the pilot can discharge flares to distract hostile missiles. These do appear on the kit although they are a little out of proportion and both front and rear sections need attention. Sheet card and tubing sections are

added to give depth. Strobe lights are represented by small round pieces of transparent plastic.

The improvements which had been made to this kit, although somewhat complex, radically enhance its appearance when finished. Yet another step is to improve the look of the jet intake areas and the exhaust nozzles and, perhaps, open up the nose section to reveal the radar 'dish'. This latter task exemplifies what was stated earlier in that there is always more to do if the modeller so choses. But having carried out extensive work on the wheel wells and cockpit, we feel we have thrown out a considerable challenge, more than enough to test the modeller's skills.

CONVERTING A JUNKERS JU 88A-4 INTO A G-6

GATHERING INFORMATION

The ever-increasing number of plastic kits produced in polystyrene, resin or by the vacuum-forming process, makes it possible that at some future date every aeroplane in history will have been recreated in model kit form somewhere in the world. Therefore there are numerous opportunities for the modeller to demonstrate acquired skills with advanced techniques applicable to any kit project.

The first step in modelling any aeroplane is to compile photographs, data and scale plans. The latter are particularly useful when modifying a kit to produce other variants. In this case the conversion of a Junkers Ju 88A-4 bomber into a G-6 night fighter was greatly assisted by the two Squadron/Signal 'In Action' titles (Nos 85 and 113) on the Ju 88 series, there being numerous additional

Sufficient information, in the form of drawings, plans and photographs in specialis publications are needed when embarking on a model conversion.

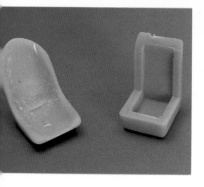

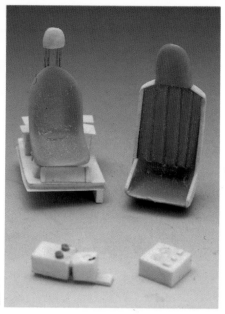

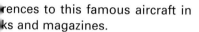
The seats in the kit are quite basic and need rubbing down and detailing.

The seats are re-shaped with a file and given side panels.

...rences to this famous aircraft in ...ks and magazines.

...he baseline model is a Ju 88A-4 ...1 Hobby Craft, a kit with an abun...ce of detail that makes conver...work that much easier. The first ...is to reconstruct and detail the ...pit interior, which includes

Plastic strip is used to add detail to all three crew seats.

modifying the seats, and to substitute the glazed nose for a solid one housing the SN-2 airborne radar set. Thin plasticard is used for the sides of the pilot's seat and copper wire for the headrest. The radio operator's seat is also built up. On the rear wall of the cockpit adjacent to the rearwards-firing machine gun

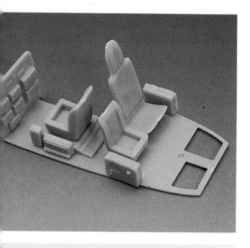

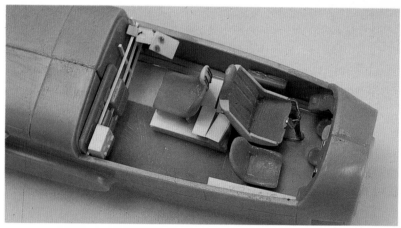

...he plasticard items are added, the copckpit ...s on a much more authentic 'feel'.

Make a thorough study of reference photographs before rebuilding the cockpit, which involves the addition of panels and control runs in plastic strip and copper wire.

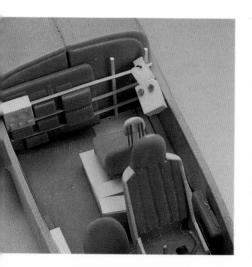

Among the cockpit modifications is to add the power units for the SN-2 Lichtenstein and FuG 227 Neptun radars. These have scopes which should be included. Note the entirely different shape of the observer's seat compared to that of the pilot's.

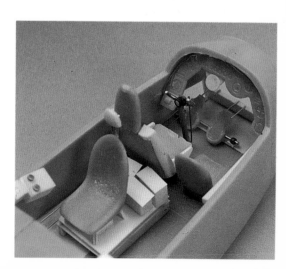

are the 'black boxes' encompassing the SN-2 and FuG-227 radar equipment and their visual indicators. These are also contructed with plastic sheet and wire.

The outline shape of both wings and tailplanes have to be changed to create the G-6 from the bomber version. Tailplane location points are filled and sanded smooth.

One of the most time-consuming steps in this conversion is the

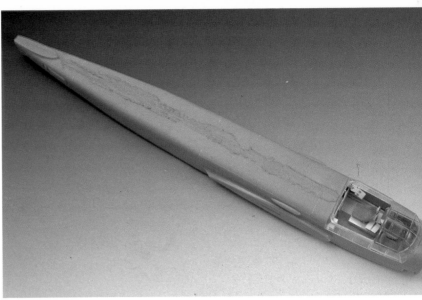

Once the cockpit modifications are complete, the fuselage halves can be joined. The is little risk of losing detail when the fuselage reshaping takes place.

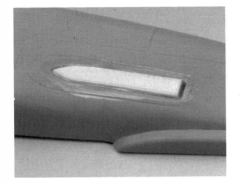

The tailplane of the Ju 88G-6 differs substantially to that of the A-4 bomber both in shape and location, so the root attachment points have to be changed.

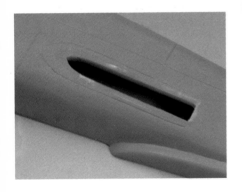

A plastic plug is used to blank off each tailplane location point.

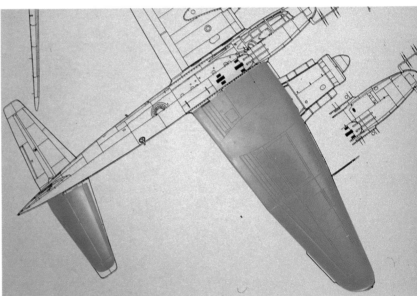

Any necessary wing modifications are checked against plans and measured.

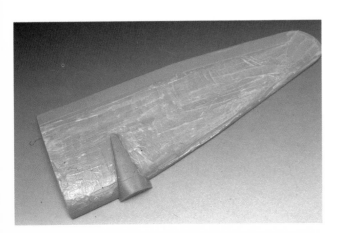

All panel lines are removed by filling with putty

The surface is smoothed off with wet & dry sandpaper wrapped around a wooden block.

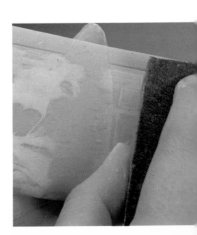

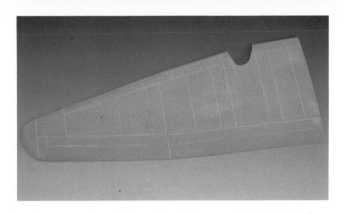

*h all original
ace detail filled,
task of
ribing new
g panel lines
begin.*

removal of all surface detail. Panel lines are sealed with putty and sanded down with wet & dry sandpaper attached to a wooden block, ready for new panels to be scribed. Aileron extensions cut from card are attached and faired into the trailing edge.

The larger G-6 tailplanes are shaped from 6-mm plasticard and built up to an aerofoil shape by glueing on layers of card. These sections are shaped with file and

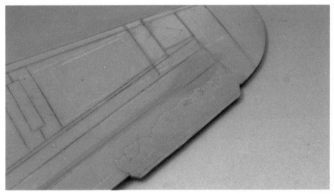

ight lines are drawn with a metal rule and punch, ensuring the part being worked on is securely firmly.

Aileron extensions are made out of card and attached.

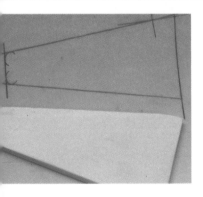

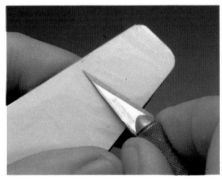

sandpaper. Measure carefully, using instruments, but do not overlook the fact that a good eye is always very useful in modelling. Smooth down and polish the new tailplanes prior to attachment to the fuselage.

Key tools and materials: lathe moulding with resin

A block of resin and a mould adapted from a canister that comes with photographic film was used to produce new engine cowlings. While this heavy plastic container is ideal, hardwood could equally well be used for the mould. Firstly, draw-

v tailplanes are built up by a series of tic sheets glued together.

Wing and tailplane leading edges are smoothed and correctly rounded.

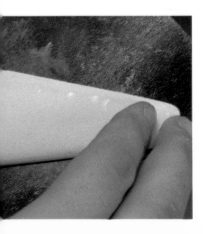

Once the main reshaping has been completed the new components are polished with sandpaper to achieve the right aerofoil section throughout the span of each tailplane.

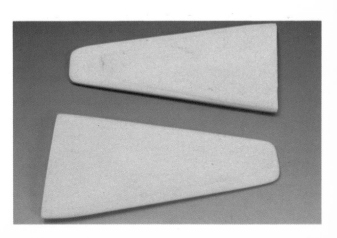

The starting point for the new Ju 88 engines is a block of resin and a film canister for the mould.

The block is held by the lathe clamps and a knife is used to mark out the detail required.

Using a chisel the cowlings are reduced to obtain the required taper and sanded smooth.

Final polishing is achieved with an abrasive attached to a wooden block working from coarse to fine grade.

The general shape of the cowling after it has been cut and polished.

The front of the new cowling is hollowed out with a small headed ch to make room for the radiator disc.

ings are made from which panel lines are inscribed onto the plastic. With the block placed on the lathe (a Unimat I in this case), the machine is started and the detail is inscribed with a firmly-held knife. Later on, a chisel is employed to reduce part of the resin block so that it adopts a slightly undersize shape. Finally, the new part has to be smoothed off with abrasive attached to a wooden block.

This type of operation on a lathe might seem daunting but it is really quite straightforward, w numerous possibilities for proc ing customised kit parts faster t with any other method. A lath very versatile with interchange accessories allowing for centra lateral drilling and milling.

The Unimat I lathe complex but vers tool useful for a range of modelling t

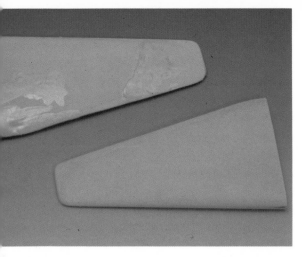

A calibrator was used to obtain the correct shape of the wings, a task that also requires a good 'eye'.

Lathes can be used with plastic, wood or aluminium, all materials now in common use in modelling.

The process of detailing the new component parts begins with drawing the general layout of the panels. A metal template with numerous photo-engraved hollow shapes is then used as a guide for a punch and scribing tool to reproduce straight lines. This remarkably flexible template can be adjusted to follow the curvature of the wings and fuselage, the detail being rescribed with a knife.

The new squared-off fin is built

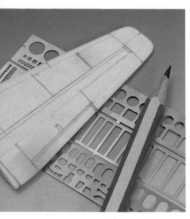

...ore any engraving of panels is ...kled, their number, shape and size ...ould be drawn accurately onto the ...stic.

A Verlinden template is invaluable when determining the correct size and depth of slots and hinges.

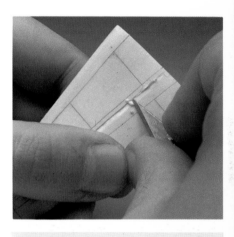

When scribing along the hinge lines that represent any movable control surface, a deeper groove will need to be made with a sharp scalpel.

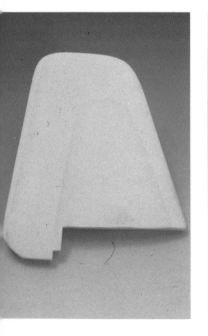

...-mm sheet of plastic was the starting ...nt for the new fin and rudder, shaped ...d smoothed off with sandpaper and ...s.

Panels and hinges are incorporated to emphasise the basic structure of the rudder.

from 7-mm plastic sheet, roughly cut out before smoothing to the correct size and shape. Wet & dry sandpaper is used to rub down the new component, a similar precedure then being followed to make the rudder. This can be separated from the fin and set at an angle, if desired. There are different procedures that can be followed to make a solid cylindrical piece; although traditionally carved from wood, such customised items can more easily be made with an epoxy putty such a Milliput. This can be shaped, scribed and rubbed down with sandpaper attached to a wooden block.

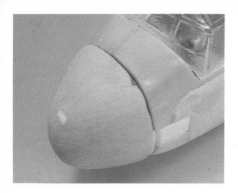

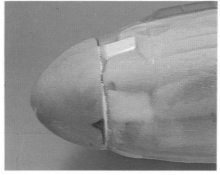

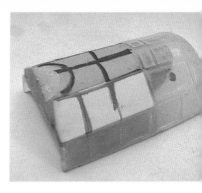

The original glazed nose section is substituted by a new solid nose made from putty.

The putty is well kneaded and moulded to the shape of the fuselage.

A new canopy framework is drawn before filling the old canopy with epo filler to obtain the basic shape that fit the fuelage cutout.

PREPARING THE COCKPIT

Although the transparent cockpit canopy supplied with the Ju 88A kit is not directly applicable to the Ju 88G variant, it can be used as a basis for vacuum-forming a new night fighter canopy. A cast of the main canopy section is taken using epoxy putty, the window area being re-drawn and sandpapered to the correct shape. When the frames of the original canopy are removed the mould is left, slimmer by the thickness of the original framing.

Once the mould is finished, it ha be glued to a wooden block for exact profile of the new canopy be built up, the dimensions hav first been thoroughly chec against plans. A countersunk bas then cut out.

*bomber kit canopy forms the basis
he new night fighter canopy, it first
g sandpapered to remove the raised
ework.*

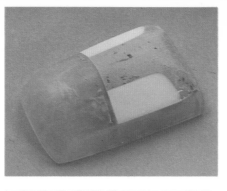

*The new mould is filled with putty and
the gaps plugged, this method making it
intentionally smaller than required.*

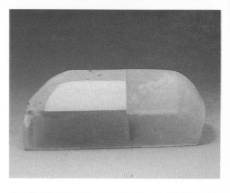

*Ready to serve as a mould for the new
canopy, the bomber canopy has now
lost its characteristic rear bulges.*

eck has to be made to ensure
the resulting male and female
es are a perfect fit, but leaving
gh room for the thickness of the
ate or other transparent plastic
ap around them. All edges have
e smoothed off before the trans-
nt sheet is placed over the

cavity. The sheet is firmly fixed with
clamps and the whole assembly
subjected to flameless heat. When it
begins to soften, the moulded piece
is fitted, thereby producing the
shape of the new canopy.

Once the transparent item is
released from its mould it has to be

measured again and trimmed,
preferably with small nail scissors
and sandpaper. The canopy frames
are cut from thin strips of plasticard,
several strips in different sizes being
required, following photographs of
the full size aircraft. The small
teardrop-shaped fairing for the

*wing 1-mm for the transparent
ring, the canopy shape is cut out of
plywood.*

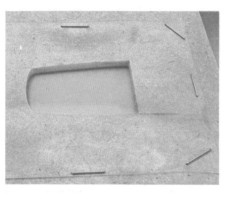

*The mould is attached to a wooden base
and the transparent material is stretched
over the female mould.*

*Heated gently, the male half is pressed
into the female half.*

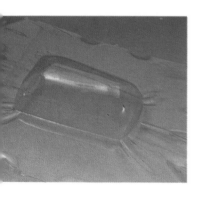

*e remoulding has been done
ectly a new canopy exactly matching
cutout in the kit fuselage halves will
it.*

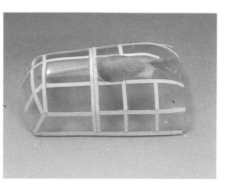

*Small strips of plasticard are used to
build up the framework of the new
canopy.*

Naxos homing device situated
above the canopy is easily made up
in putty. Flattened off on its lower
edge it is glued into position at the
rear of the canopy.

To build the nacelle a block of sandwiched plastic sheets is prepared.

The sandwich is clamped firmly for good bonding.

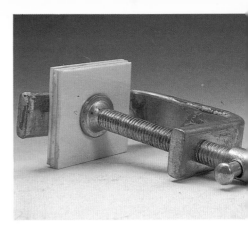

The block is smoothed off with a knife approximating the final shape and finished with files and fine grade sandpaper.

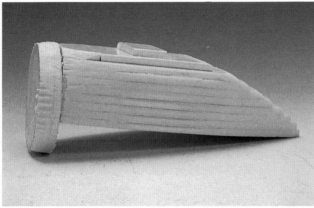

VACUUM-FORMING PREPARATION

Each engine nacelle is also re duced using the vacuum-form method and, for this, block plastic slightly larger than the dimensions are required. nacelle is made by glueing se sheets of 2-mm plasticard toge to make a sandwich. This is trimmed to the approximate s and length and finally smoo down with file and sandpaper u

Mounted on a wooden block, any gaps are conveniently filled with putty and polished until the surface is very smooth.

The female mould, shaped to the correct dimensions, is then prepared.

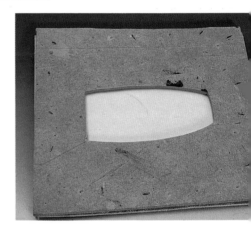

Nacelle sections are cast by following the same procedure as for the cockpit canopy.

Trimmed almost to the exact dimensions, some final honing and test-fitting may be required.

engine and nacelle are joined with an intervening firewall tion made from plastic sheet. This is adjusted and sandpa-ed to shape.

Putty is used to fair in the new sections to the kit wing, the joint being sanded to shape.

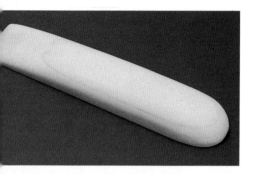

The ventral fuse-lage gun gondola is made from plastic sheet, cut to size and glued in posi-tion. The cartridge case ejector slots are cut out and cleaned up with a fine file.

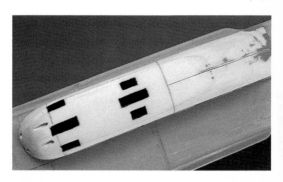

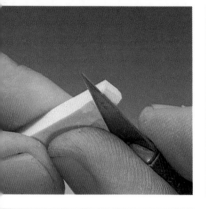

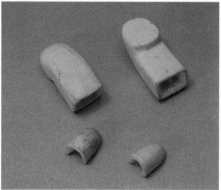

air intakes are built up, starting with nall square of plasticard.

Other small intakes are similarly shaped with file and sandpaper.

mates snugly with the wing and engine cowling.

All remaining holes and gaps are filled with putty, the entire sub-assembly then being given a final polish. The vacuum-formed male section is formed first, this being slightly smaller to allow for the plastic 'coating' it will receive. Glued into the base cavity the female piece is prepared by tracing the exact shape onto paper. Cutting out is with a marquetry saw, 1-mm larger than required so that it forms a 'skin' over the female half.

Once the vacuum-formed compo-nents are ready, they are trimmed and glued to the wing, any

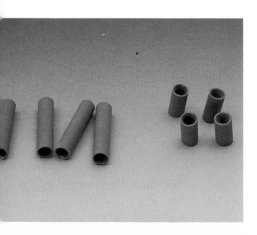

The flame damper exhaust pipes are made from plastic tubing.

A view of one engine assembly, almost entirely custom-made.

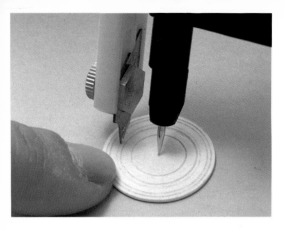

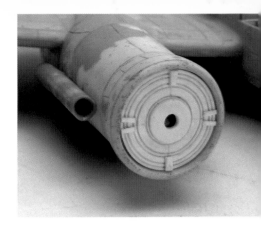

remaining gaps being filled with putty.

The engines are mated up with the new nacelles and the kit wing, filling the join at the top with putty. Sandpapered and polished, the new surfaces are ready for scribing.

The single ventral gun gondola is constructed from plasticard and detailed with reference to plans and photographs Additional items such as air intakes are sculpted with scalpel and files, building up small squares of plastic.

Brackets for the radar aerials are drawn to scale on 1-mm thick plasticard.

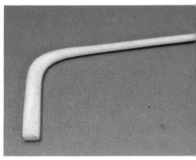

With their edges smoothed off the ae— brackets are finally shaped and sande to the correct cross-section.

regular distances apart. A hole for the propeller pin is drilled before fitting the radiator sections into the front of each engine cowling.

Once the circular radiator secti— have been scribed they are fit— into the cowlings. The radar aer— now need to be drawn onto

Flame damping exhaust pipes were fitted to Ju 88Gs and these are fabricated from plastic tubing. To detail them, a small tube cutting tool can be employed to clamp and rotate them with a fin point touching the surface. At the front of each nacelle the annular radiator can be represented by scribing concentric circles into a plastic disc. A precision scriber will ensure that the rings remain at

...m plasticard, cut out and sanded
...hape. These plastic sections are
...itioned ready to take the dipoles
...ch are made from hypodermic
...dle sections and thin wire.

... will be useful to use airscrew
...nners from other 1/48 scale kits
...h as the Ju 87 or Dornier Do 335,
...vailable. Alternatively these can
...vacuum-formed.

...he male section of the spinner is
...de by shaping a wooden dowel
...htly smaller in cross section than
...uired. The female half starts as a

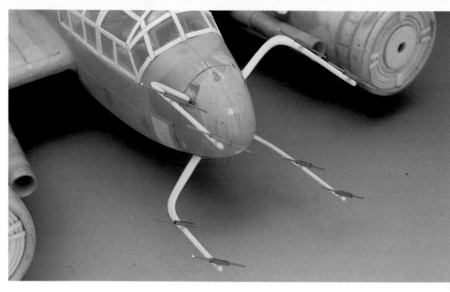

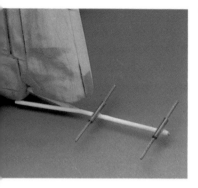

*...aerial under the rudder also has to
...ade from similar materials.*

Location of the aerials of the SN-2 Lichtenstein radar. Each arm carries two vertical aerials made from hypodermic needles and wire.

In lieu of finding suitable spinners in the spares box these can be be vacuum-formed or turned up from wood.

In this case the spinners were made by the vacuum-forming process described earlier.

Overall view of the Ju 88G-6 with the new components in place. The degree of fabrication necessary with such an ambitious conversion is under-standably high.

If they are available, spinners from a 1/48 scale Do 335 or two Ju 87s can be used on the Ju 88G.

disc to the exact size in 1-mm plasti-card. Heating this and mating it with the wooden conical end results in a perfect spinner shape to take the propeller.

The tail warning radar aerial is made from plastic rod with a 'V' shape cut to take the horizontal dipoles made from wire.

The cockpit rear gun is located in a circular armoured glass cupola. This latter is traced onto 2-mm plastic sheet (or two 1-mm sections joined together). A hole is made in the clear plastic with a needle file and shaped to take the gun. Finally, the horseshoe-shaped fairing is up in putty and sanded to shape.

The gondola guns are made from plastic tubing or hypoden needles, these also being used a alternative to wire for the s aerials located on the wings fuselage.

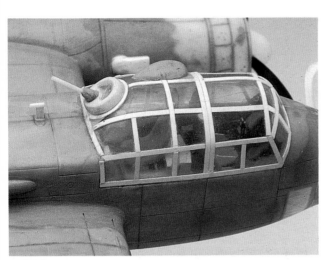

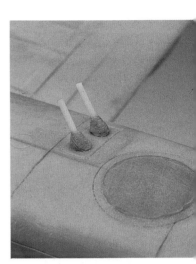

The machine gun shield at the rear of the cockpit is made from 2-mm plasti-card.

In the centre of the fuselage top the barrels of a twin 'Schrage Musik' upwards-firing cannon installation have been added.

The model has been completed with the landing gear in the retracted position; note the size of the new engine nacelles and the ventral cannon gondola.

SCRATCHBUILDING AN AIRCRAFT

st World War aeroplanes are very attractive to many people and, given their small size, they can be built in a large scale without their dimensions being unwieldy.

e Roland C.II model described here is to 1/35 scale, the popular size for tanks and AFVs which means that it could easily be incorporated into dioramas which include figures. All the materials necessary to scratch build this model have been described in the previous pages and this is in the nature of a final exercise, applying acquired knowledge and expertise.

e Roland presents something of a challenge due to the characteristic fish shape of the selage and the need to build up the entire wing structure. Also, the 'fish scale' colour heme chosen to finish the aircraft is not the simplest, so here too there is the need for a careful, planned approach.

ROLAND C.II 'WALFISCH'

Although not one of the most famous fighters of the First World War, the Roland C.II represented an important technological advance, particularly in the design and construction of the wooden semi-monocoque fuselage, which was in marked contrast to contemporary design. Another feature that attracts modellers is the interesting fish scale camouflage which gave the aircraft its nickname. Construction follows a design approach typical of the period and one adopted for numerous aircraft types then and in the decades following the war. The starting point is to determine the outline shape, the wing ribs and the fuselage cross sections. A scale plan will reveal these but in the event that a plan is not to hand, these sections can be drawn up by taking a centre point for

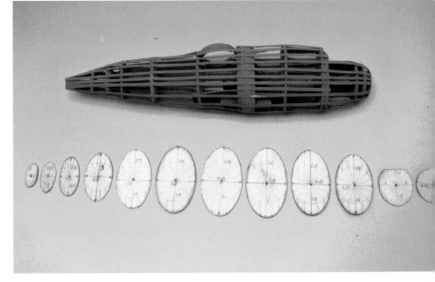

The fuselage structure shown with the cross sections that are required to build it up from scratch.

RUCTURE OF THE FUSELAGE

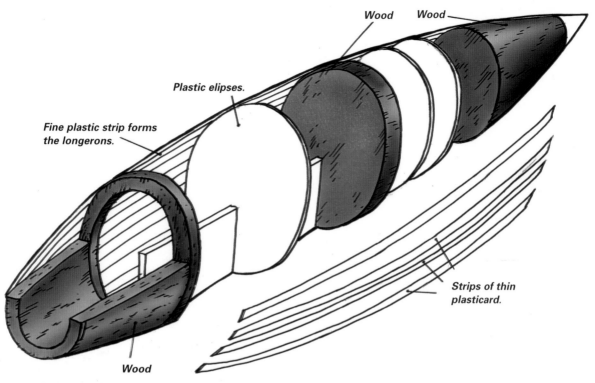

Wood

Wood

Plastic elipses.

Fine plastic strip forms
the longerons.

Strips of thin
plasticard.

Wood

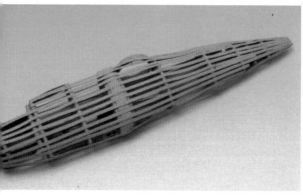

...tion of the plastic and wooden sections and partial lining
...plastic strip.

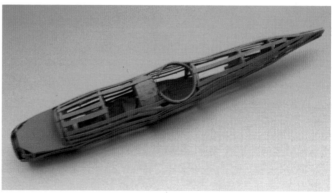

Cockpit cutouts for the pilots and observer are made in the
fuselage top.

...propeller is made from fine
...ood.

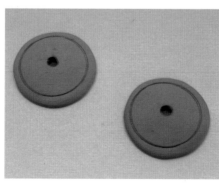

The wheels were adapted from plastic
tokens.

the basic measurements.

The easiest way to obtain an elipse is with a compass and dividers with measurements taken from the centre point.

The elipses are cut out of plasticard and located in their appropriate place in the fuselage. A longitudinal stringer representing the fuselage centreline will be required, this being made from 1-mm plastic sheet. In addition, a radial slot in the vertical axis reaching into the centre is made in each eliptical section. Using this method the stringer can be fitted and fixed accurately. At the nose and tail, small elipses are replaced by solid wooden pieces to

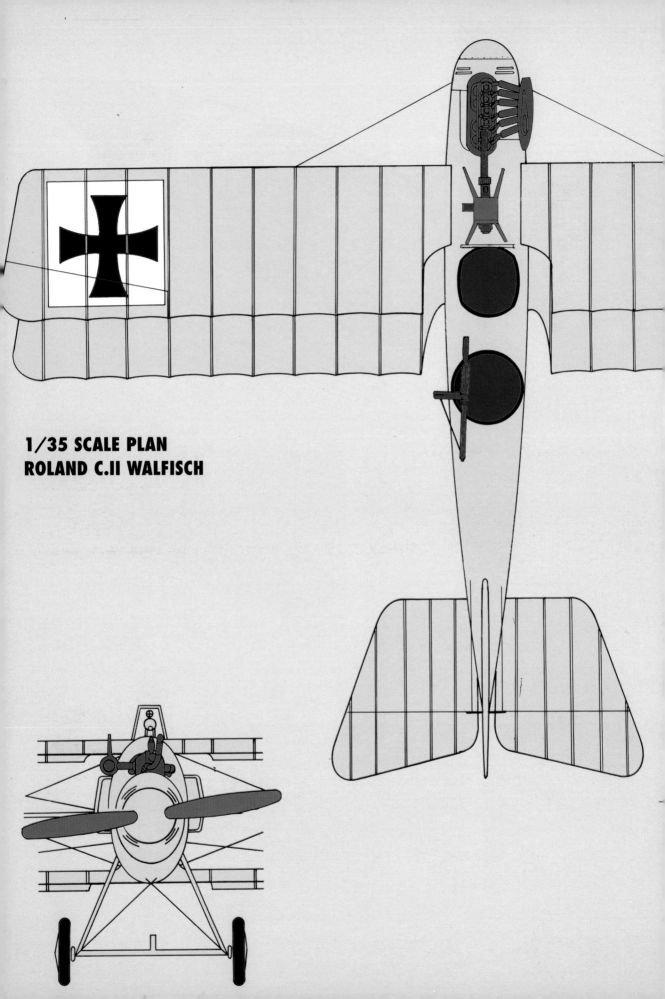

1/35 SCALE PLAN
ROLAND C.II WALFISCH

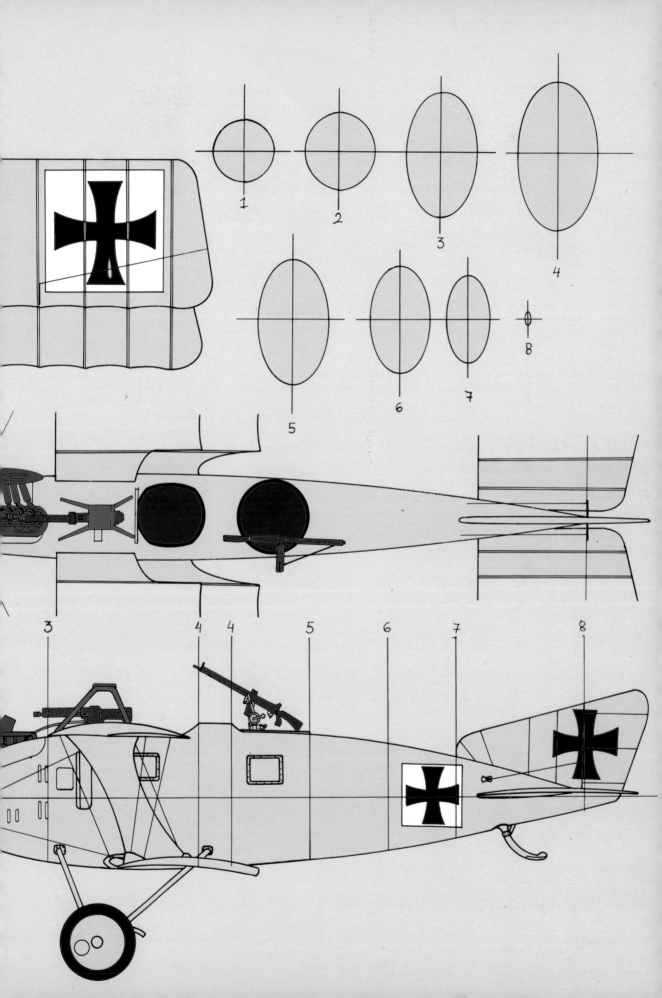

COVERING THE FUSELAGE

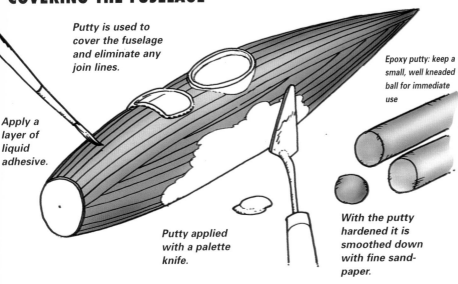

Putty is used to cover the fuselage and eliminate any join lines.

Apply a layer of liquid adhesive.

Epoxy putty: keep a small, well kneaded ball for immediate use

Putty applied with a palette knife.

With the putty hardened it is smoothed down with fine sand-paper.

With the putty hardened, it is smooth down with sand paper.

provide rigidity and strength.

Once all the eliptical fuselage sections have been aligned, they are glued in place and the model is ready to have its plastic strip outer covering applied. This will not need to be perfectly smooth at this stage,

an even surface being all that is necessary. Even some gaps are permissable at the ends of the strips. Once the covering is complete the fuselage window openings and the crew access must be made. The entire assembly will receive a final

sanding but to secure the join coating of liquid adhesive can be applied.

With the basic construc complete the whole surface is g a generous coating of epoxy p using a palette knife to obtain

Small surface deformities and cracks are filled and smoothed down, the putty being reapplied in any areas that have suffered filler shrinkage.

Fuselage windows are made by drilling a series of holes and filing the edges smooth.

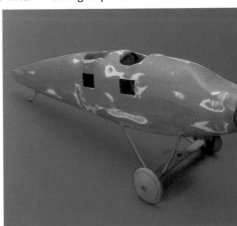

The landing gear is made from thick wire for strength and rigidity.

Ensure that the spacer bar is strong enough to bear the we of the aircraft.

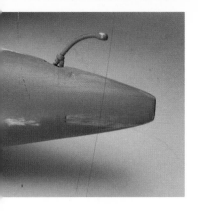

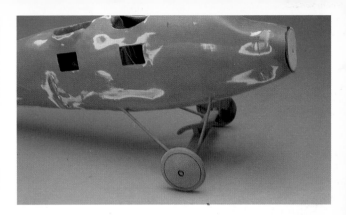

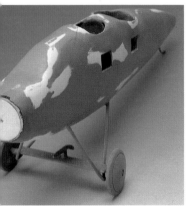

Wire is also used to make the tailskid, this being firmly anchored to one of the solid wooden fuselage sections.

In the centre of the landing gear is a characteristically curved balance.

The nose section is completely circular, tapering down to the propeller spinner.

Small windows, locating points and cooling slots are made from plastic strip.

Each radiator comprises a metal grille stuck to a fairing and covered with a plastic lining.

rs.

utty can be smoothed on with a
h and water and sanded before
cond layer is applied, if neces-
. Each layer is rubbed down
oughly with a flexible abrasive.
n the smoothing and polishing
ess is complete, a base coat of
t in a neutral colour, such as
, is applied. This serves as a last
k for irregularities in the finish
hat a final rub down can be
ed out as necessary.

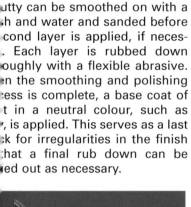

*circular cone-shaped sections glued
ther go to make the propeller
ner, any gaps being filled with putty.*

General view of the fuselage with the main details completed and locating holes made for the wing struts.

CONSTRUCTION AND REFINING THE WING SHAPE

Plasticard wing section

Sandpaper.

Using a half-round file.

Refinging the wing aerofoil

Reducing thickness with a rough file.

Intermediate smoothing.

Sandpaper held ove cylindrical or oval v block makes this pa the work easier.

Compare the original 3-mm plasticard section and a partially formed and smoothed wing.

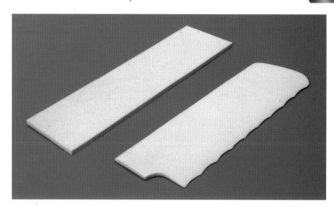

CONSTRUCTING THE WINGS

The mainplanes of the Roland present a few problems owin their scalloped trailing edges. way to reproduce this feature scratch-built kit is to start with mm thick plastic rectangle. Ar with the dimensions of each v the straight leading edges are out with a rule and the curved between each rib cut round w marquetry saw.

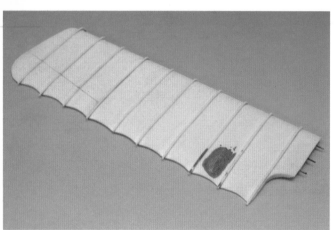

Plastic rods glued over previously drawn rib lines.

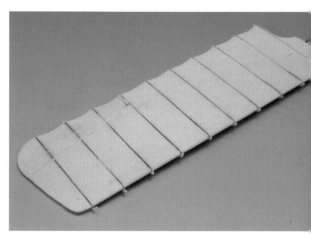

Rods are applied to all wing ribs. Leading and trailing edge are sanded smooth.

Dry run check for correct wing dihedral angle

Each leading and trailing e section is treated separatel general smoothing down b achieved with a coarse file be finishing with wet & dry sandpa The next step is very delicate requires constant checking ensure uniformity and to recr the subtle concave form of the e wing area. The initial rough sha is done with a half-round file.

48

For strong joints, metal guides are introduced.to fix the wings.

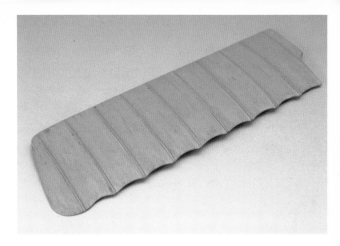

Putty is applied to the wing surface which is then covered with fine fabric that has been wetted, to create an authentic texture.

...he appearance of longitudinal ...ion should decrease from the ...re towards the wing extremities ... gradual fashion, avoiding the ...earance of 'gutters'. Fine grade ...dpaper wrapped around a cylin-...al or oval wooden block is used ... finishing. Once the general ...pe of the wings has been ...ned, fine plastic rod is attached ...g each rib line. These rods are ...led, with putty being applied ...g the lateral edges where neces-...

...trailing edge cut-out is required ...re each lower mainplane joins

It is advisable to cover the entire wing surface with the wet fabric strips so that irregulari- ties are avoided.

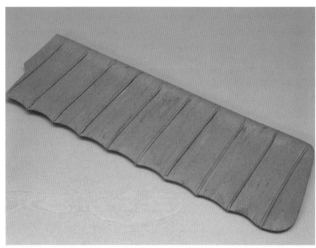

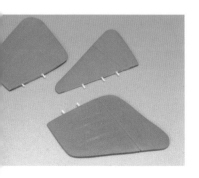

The set of four wings showing the rib and fabric simu- lation on all surfaces.

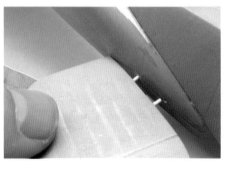

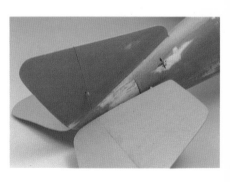

...rudder and tailplane do not require ...nuch attention as the wings, only a ...ling and trailing edge shaping being ...uired.

A metal anchor is also incorporated into the tailplane joints for strength.

The three tail surfaces in position along with the locating point for the bracing wires.

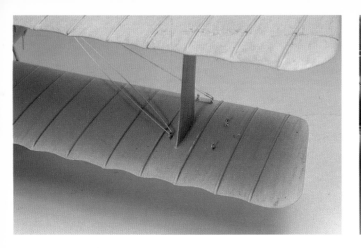

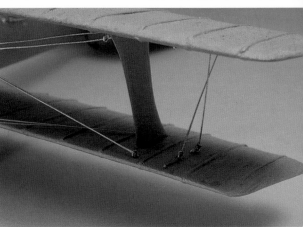

Test fitting the wing bracing wires to check tension.

Aileron movement on the Roland was also achieved by wire tension.

the fuselage. Alignment of the lower wings is made easier by inserting metal rods into the attachment holes.

The centre section of the upper wing is fabricated from plasticard, following the dimensions given on the plan. The tailplanes and rudder are made in the same way, the advantage here being that all the surfaces are 'flat'.

Positioned along the fuselage sides is a series of small protuberances including the pick-up points for bracing wires. Again plastic strip is employed to reproduce these and the frames of the observation windows. Transparent acetate doubles for the 'glass' areas and Plastruct can be used to add detail to

the machine gun mounts adjace both cockpits. The propeller is up from layers of very thin plyw which are cut and sanded to sh the sandwiched layers eventu giving an authentic, laminated w effect. The radiators need to ha metal grille effect both front rear.

The   radiators   are   sha

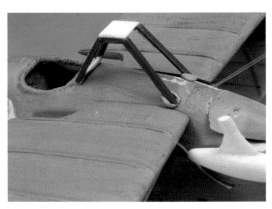

Plastruct was used to make the shield for the LMG 08/15 machine gun.

The exhaust pipe fairing is made from a small square of plasticard rounded and shaped with file and sandpaper.

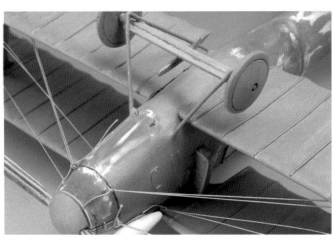

Dry run to check length of bracing wires from the nose to the wings.

Prior to installing the engine, a putty bulkhead has to be located on the front fuselage and drilled for location purpos

1/35 SCALE MERCEDES D-III ENGINE. *Top view and right and left side profiles.*

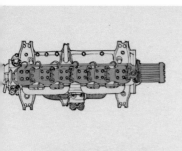

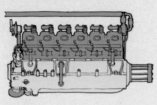

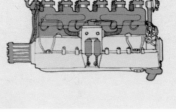

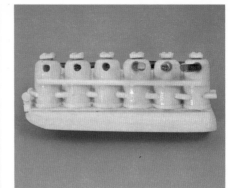

Plastic tube and rod is used to make the cylinders.

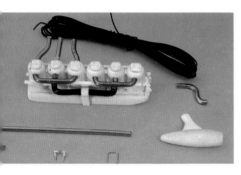

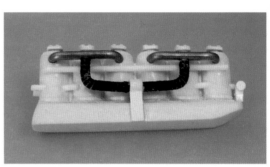

Inlet and exhaust manifolds are fabricated from thick copper wire, with thin wire being used for the spark plugs.

according to the scale plan and positioned after plastic strip is used to cover the grille area.

THE ENGINE

The Mercedes D-III engine that powered the Roland C.II is a relatively complex component in modelling terms, comprising six cylinders set into a block with accompanying valve guides, exhaust manifold and main shaft

...part of the engine is visible when ...ted, so the lower sections can be ...red.

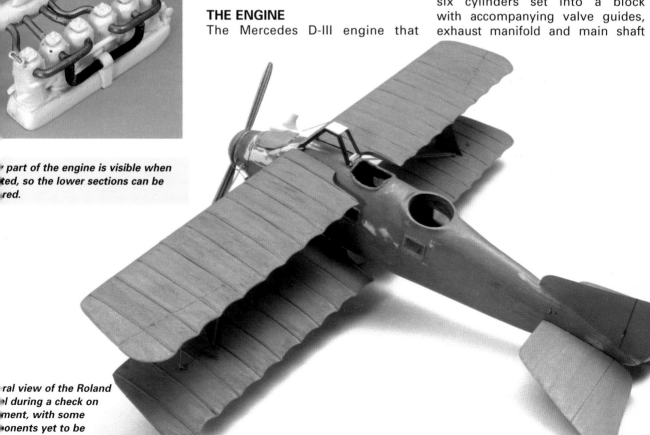

...ral view of the Roland ...l during a check on ...ment, with some ...onents yet to be ...d.

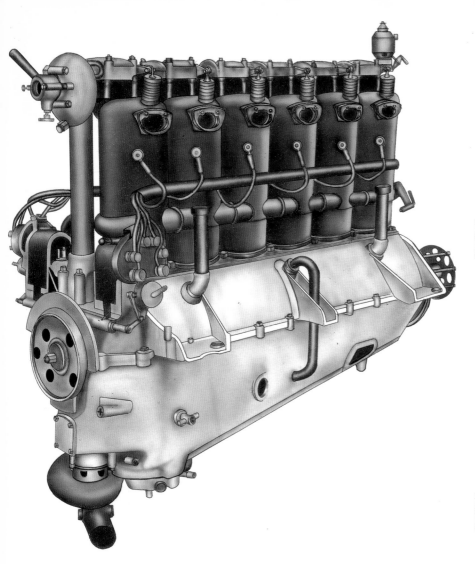

Test-fitting the engine in its location.

drive.

Only the exposed upper half of the engine needs to be built. Again the dimensions shown on the plan were checked before a block of plastic was cut to size. The cylinders were made from 5-mm diameter plastic tubing over which is placed a 2-mm domed top part, sanded to give the charac-teristic shape.

The manifold is simulated by thick wire bent round with pointed head pliers; the remainder of engine detail is made from pl strip and tubing, cut and sha accordingly.

Fine copper wire is used to s late the spark plug leads.

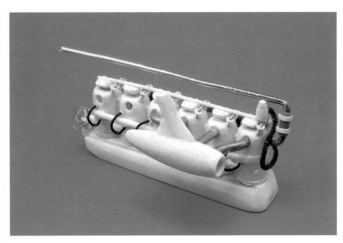

Close-up view of the right side of the engine showing wiring and the exhaust fairing.

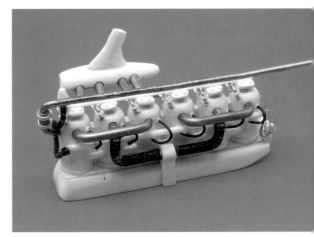

Left side, showing valve sleeves and the inlet manifold.

...ate is used to make the windscreen, which is framed in
...plastic strip.

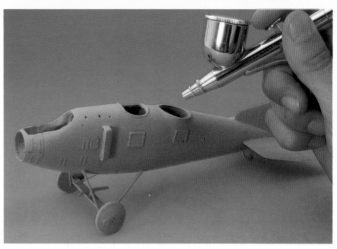

The first coat of sea grey acrylic is applied.

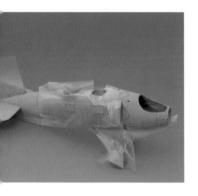

...ably masked for the second colour,
...blue is applied over the grey.

...of the tape masking applied to the
...side of the fuselage to simulate the
...scale camouflage.

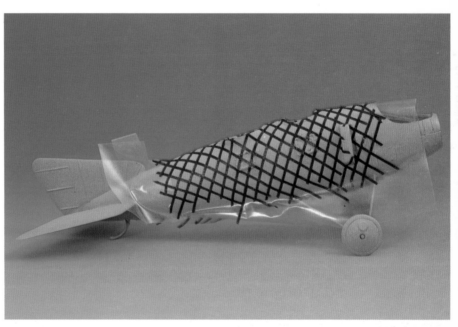

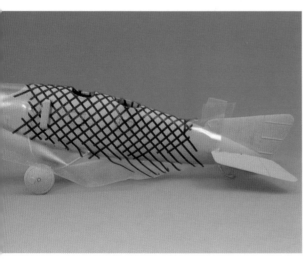

...hand side: care must be taken when applying the tape
...to maintain symmetry.

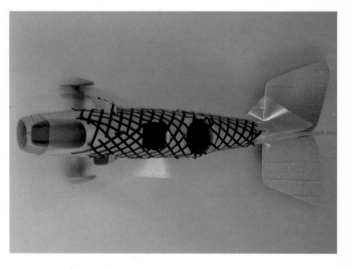

The squares on the fuselage are regular, there being some
variation in pattern only around the nose.

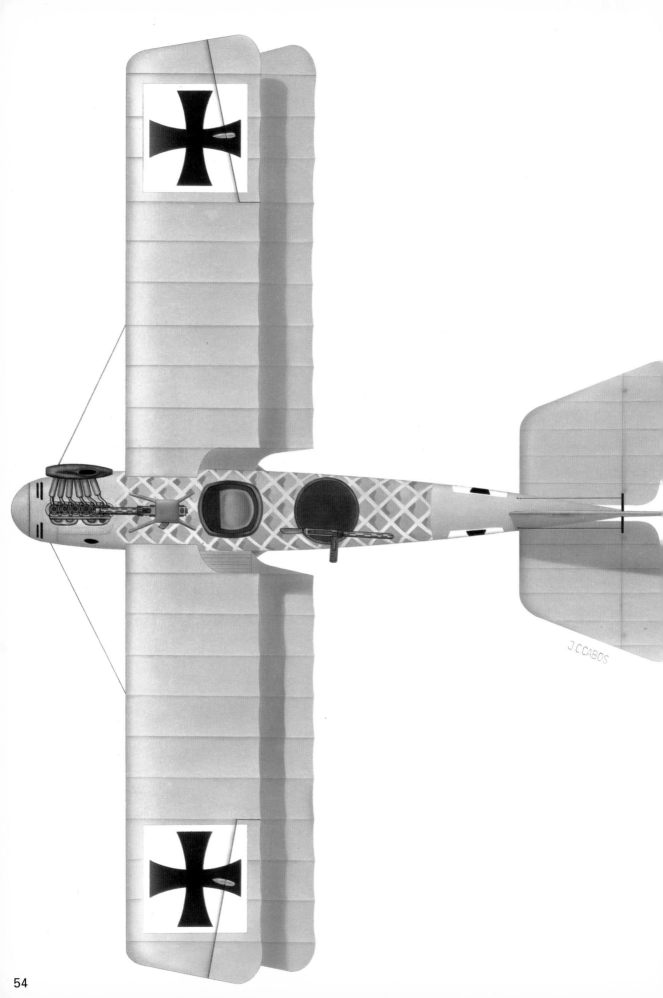

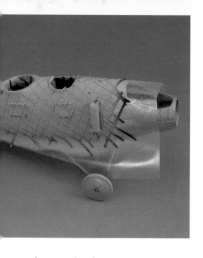

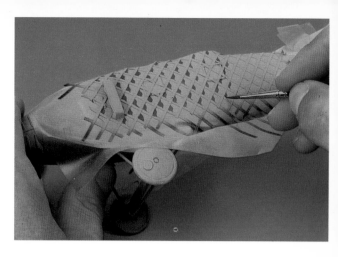

...aust is made in two sections,
...the manifold plate cut from a
...ll square of plastic, smoothed
...polished along the edges. Later,
...le is drilled and filed to take the
...aust pipe.

PAINTING AND DECORATION

The colour scheme chosen is that which typified the aircraft's nickname. The soft tones are applied to duplicate the scales of a fish, which calls for careful masking of the model. Acrylic colours were applied with an airbrush, these being a light sea grey base coat on the fuselage and rudder followed by light blue for the wings, part of the rudder and the rear fuselage.

Depth is achieved on the scales by mixing medium blue and white. The 'shadow' of each one is applied

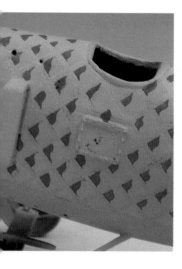

When lifting the
masking strips, all
outlines should be
well defined,
although some
retouching may be
necessary.

The right-hand side
of the model
showing the inter-
esting fish scale
effect, achieved as
previously
described.

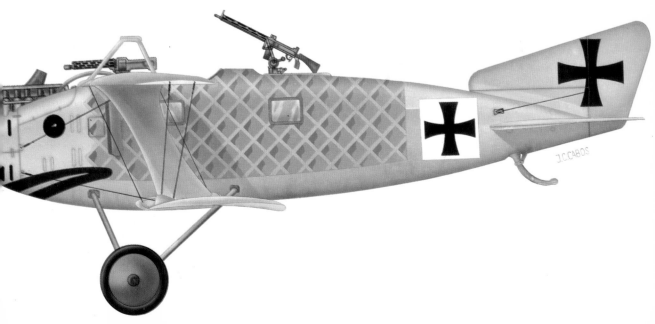

J.C.CABOS

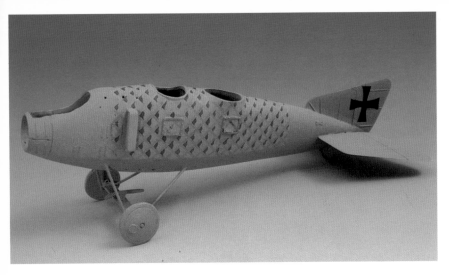

Left-hand side again, with the regular scales well proportioned.

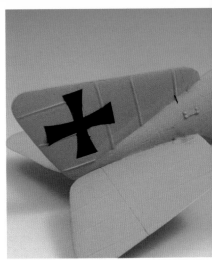

The tail cross is painted with the help of adhesive mask.

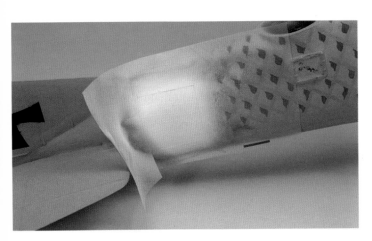

The white ground for the cross is masked off.

Measuring the correct distance from the tailplane, the fuselage cross is sprayed on.

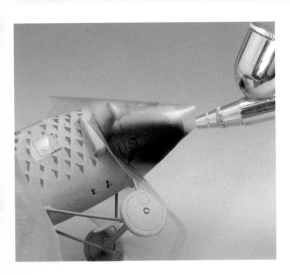

In making a mask for the 'sharkmouth', allowance has to be made for the curvature of the fuselage.

Care with the mask will result in a convincing mouth decoration.

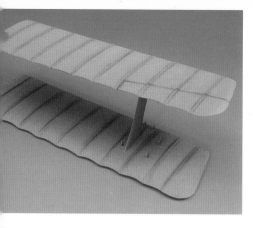

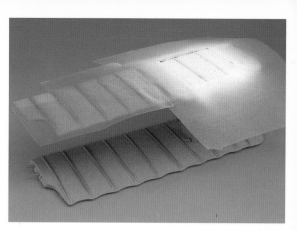

The wing ribs are given false shadows to enhance depth.

The method of applying the wing crosses is the same as that for the fuselage.

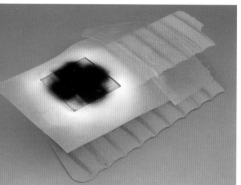

Mask well out from the white crosses to avoid accidentally over-spraying the camouflage.

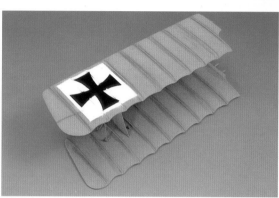

in dark blue with a small amount of white added to it.

Masks are needed for the national insignia crosses on their white square backgrounds. They are traced from the plans (and enlarged slightly for those on the undersides) and cut out of adhesive masking tape.

Care should be taken to trim the mask to the correct size to reproduce the scales, taking account of the slight variations in shape and width on each side of the fuselage. In total, the scales cover an area of

w of the model with most
e detail work completed.

Painting the Mercedes engine starts with an overall coat of aluminium, sprayed on.

Transparent sepia ink is used to highlight the top half, which includes the cylinders and spark plugs.

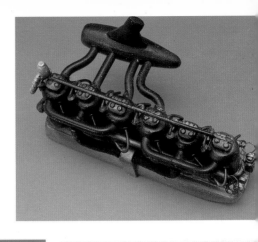

ten centimetres.

The base camouflage on the fuselage is divided into fourteen sections each 7-mm wide on both sides. The masking tape is stretched over the fuselage in diagonal lines in two directions until all areas are covered in a criss-cross pattern.

A reddish tone, simulating a burnt effect, is applied to the cylinder heads, the wiring is yellow.

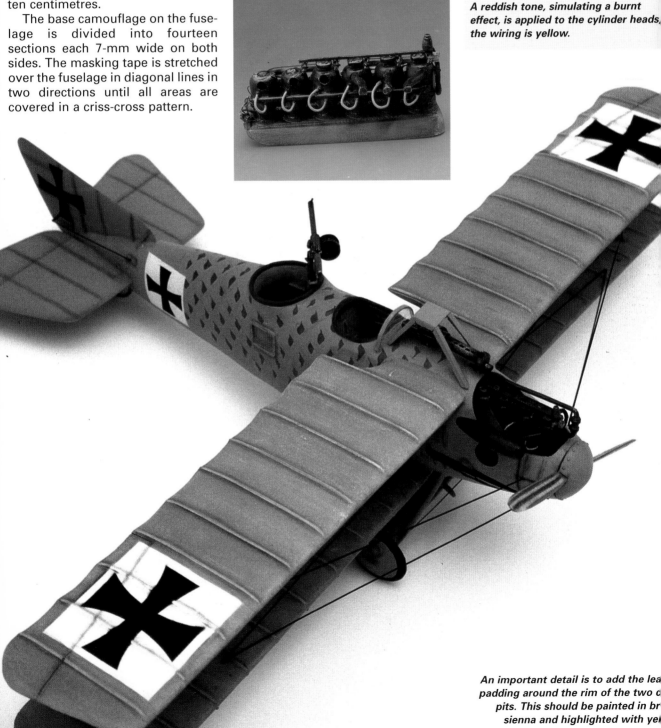

An important detail is to add the lea padding around the rim of the two c pits. This should be painted in br sienna and highlighted with ye

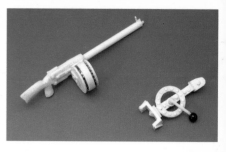

Armament of the Roland C.II consisted of a fixed Maxim 08/15 machine gun, the famous Spandau, for the pilot, and a Parabellum fired by the observer, using a flexible mounting.

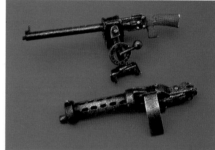

h the engine in position the colour can be highlighted. Sepia is the dominant colour ough the exhaust pipes can be treated with extra red to create a rusty, burnt earance.

Dry brushing the wing with the main colour lightened with white will bring out the fabric texture.

Distances are carefully measured before fitting the bracing wires.

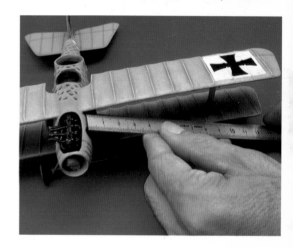

all holes are made to locate the ends of the wires.

The wire is stretched to the correct tension before it is cut and glued with cyanoacrylate.